# FACT OR FAKE?

# THE TRUTH ABOUT
# SPORT

**ANNABEL SAVERY**

WAYLAND

First published in Great Britain in 2022 by Wayland
Copyright © Hodder and Stoughton Limited, 2022

Produced for Wayland by
White-Thomson Publishing Ltd
www.wtpub.co.uk

Editor: Annabel Savery
Series Designer: Rocket Design (East Anglia) Ltd

HB ISBN: 978 1 5263 1850 3
PB ISBN: 978 1 5263 1851 0

Wayland
An imprint of
Hachette Children's Group
Part of Hodder & Stoughton
Carmelite House
50 Victoria Embankment
London EC4Y 0DZ

An Hachette UK Company

www.hachettechildrens.co.uk

Printed in China

Picture acknowledgements:
Shutterstock: The Toon Company 3, Don Purcell 4, kintomo 5, autumnn 6, Farah Sadikhova 7, denniro 8, BNP Design Studio 9, Lyudmyla Kharlamova 10 l, Shchasny 10 r, Sararoom Design 11, 21 and 94, PaintDoor 12, vectoric 13, GSapphire 14–15, Vector Tradition 16, chompoo 17, Monster_Design 18, tetsuu 19, Elala 20, miniwide 22, Moz87 23, Antonov Maxim 24, Shtonado 25, Ichestnut 26 r, Giuseppe_R 26 l, elmm 27, onot 28, Daria Falcon 29, Alex Tsuper 30, lineartestpilot 31, falisdeka 32, Alluvion Stock 33, bsd 34, AmitDebnath 35, Sabelskaya 36, bioraven 37, Scc.comics 38–39 (boxers) and 57, Aluna1 38–39 (ring), yellowline 40, MarijaPiliponyte 41, anastasia.alevtina 42, Eka Panova 44, MoQcCa 45, Drawlab19 46–47, ridhobadal 48, olllikeballoon 49, daseugen 50, happyday337 51, Alan Benge 52, Miceking 53, Anton Brand 54, display intermaya 55, dixxo 56, mijatmijatovic 58, 60 and 86, babayuka 59, HitToon 61, 76 and 93, Snap2Art 62, Yoko Design 63, Artskrin 64–65 (castle), Cory Thoman 66 and 94, IrynMerry 67, Lunarus 67 and 93 (paint splat), Les Perysty 68, art of line 69, RocketBeam 70, Luciano Cosmo 71, Lorthois Yuliya 72, Kamieshkova 73, St Aiko 74, Matija Jovanovic 75, JosepPerianes 77, Fandorina Liza 78, John T Takai 79, Liliya Kulianionak 80, okili77 81, AnggaR3ind 82, kstudija 83, Rauf Aliyev 84 (volleyball), zizi_mentos 84 (snow), art of line 85, Anastasiia Cherviak 87, Ron and Joe 88, Bulgn 89, aksol 90, kyoko AMK 91.

All design elements from Shutterstock.

# CAN YOU SEPARATE THE FACTS FROM THE FAKES?

**WORM CHARMING IS AN ACTUAL SPORT.**

**DEFINITELY!**

**SNURFING IS A POPULAR WINTER SPORT.**

**NO WAY!**

**WEARING RED MIGHT HELP YOU TO WIN.**

**WHAT??**

**THE LONGEST EVER BOXING MATCH LASTED 110 ROUNDS AND TOOK 7 HOURS.**

**REALLY?!**

Read on to find out the reality behind popular match myths and mind-blowing sport stories. Discover the truth behind it all and then dazzle your teammates, friends and family with bizarre, hilarious and totally winning sport facts!

Have I won or lost?

# YOU CAN WIN A RACE BY COMING LAST

To win a 'backyard ultra' race you have to run for longer than anyone else. Each runner's goal is to be the last one still in the race when all others have dropped out!

## TELL ME MORE

When Big Dog's Backyard Ultra launched in Tennessee, USA, in 2017, it was the first race of its kind. Runners must complete a 6.7 km loop every hour for as long as they can. At the start of each hour, runners gather in the starting box – any runner not present is eliminated.

## BACKYARD WINNERS

The 2020 Backyard Ultra race took place all over the world due to the Covid 19 pandemic. Courtney Dauwater won the US race with a run of 68 hours that covered 455 km. Karel Sabbe won the International race, covering 502 km in 75 hours!

VERDICT

**Fact**

4

# GOLF

## STANDS FOR GENTLEMEN ONLY, LADIES FORBIDDEN

### FACT OR FAKE?

The idea that GOLF stands for 'gentlemen only, ladies forbidden' is just a rumour. Mentions of it date back only to around 1997, whereas records of the sport and term 'golf' date back to the 1400s.

### TELL ME MORE

The term 'golf' is mentioned in a Scottish document from 1457, banning the sport along with football. It may have been that Scottish men were letting their archery skills slip in favour of golf and football. At the time, threat of invasion was constant so fun sports were banned by King James II!

VERDICT
Fake

5

# WEARING RED COULD HELP YOU TO WIN

## FACT OR FAKE?

Some research has shown that teams wearing red may be more likely to win! Could it be down to our natural instinct that sees red as a colour of dominance and aggression?

## TELL ME MORE

While some research looks at the way we react to red, other researchers believe that players are more visible in red. Still others think that the advantage comes from the way the referee sees players in red. The jury's out, but the reds are in!

VERDICT
Fact

# OLYMPIC GOLD MEDALS ARE MADE OF GOLD

## FACT OR FAKE?

At the 1912 Olympics in Stockholm, Sweden, the gold medals were actually made of solid gold. However, today, Olympic medals contain just 6 grams of gold.

## TELL ME MORE

Medals are made to the International Olympic Committee guidelines which require 92.5% silver to be used and a minimum of 6 grams of gold. The World Gold Council estimated in 2012 that if all the medals from the Olympics were made of solid gold, the cost would be around $40 million.

### RECYCLED WINNERS

At the 2016 Rio games, medals also contained elements of recycled electronic equipment as a demonstration of Brazil's commitment to sustainability.

## VERDICT
## Fake

# SKI BALLET WAS ONCE A POPULAR SPORT

## FACT OR FAKE?

Swishing down the slopes, doing jumps, flips and spins, with costumes and music: this was ski ballet. Popular in the 1970s, it was a rebel movement led by those breaking away from rigid skiing rules!

## TELL ME MORE

Ski ballet first featured in the Winter Olympics in Canada in 1988. It also appeared at the 1992 games but was dropped afterwards as the crowds were more drawn to the snowboarding events.

### ACROSKI

Ski ballet is now called acroski but still struggles for fans. There have been no formal competitions since 2000.

**VERDICT**
**Fact**

8

# ATHLETES GET DUNKED IN AN ICE BATH IF THEY LOSE

## FACT OR FAKE?

Following a tough match, tennis player Andy Murray is known to hop into a bath of ice water. Basketball star LeBron James has jumped in one, as have athletes competing in everthing from athletics to football.

## TELL ME MORE

Many athletes are fans of ice baths, using them whether they win or lose. It's not only sports people who are fans: Lady Gaga has one after big shows and so do some ballet dancers. Ice baths are supposed to soothe tired muscles by reducing inflammation and encouraging repair. However, the science is still undecided about whether this is the best treatment.

**VERDICT**

**Fake**

# BASKETBALL BASKETS WERE ORIGINALLY FOR PEACHES

## TELL ME MORE

To keep his students busy in bad weather, Naismith nailed his peach-baskets on to balconies 3 m from the ground. The students formed teams and tried to get a ball into the baskets. The first game was chaos, but the students wanted to play again. Naismith brought in more rules, and basketball was born.

## FACT OR FAKE?

When Canadian-American physical education teacher James Naismith found a pair of peach-collecting baskets and hung them at each end of a gymnasium in 1891, he had no idea the sport he invented would go on to become a worldwide phenomenon.

**VERDICT**
## Fact

# TENNIS RACKET STRINGS ARE MADE FROM CAT GUTS

## FACT OR FAKE?

Guts yes, cats' ... no. Some tennis racket strings are made from the intestines (guts) of cows. Gut string is strong and springy. It takes two cows to make enough string for one racket!

## TELL ME MORE

There is a reason for this misunderstanding: there was a stringed instrument in the Middle Ages (c. 1100–1500 CE) that sounded like a cat's yowl when played; it was known as a 'cat'. The instrument's strings were made from 'gut' or animal intestines. As more uses were found for the string it became known as 'catgut'.

## NEW Vs OLD

Many tennis players think 'natural' or gut strings are best, but they are expensive and less durable, so most people use strings made of polyester.

## VERDICT
. . . . . . . . . . . . . .
**Fake**

11

# BOXER WLADIMIR KLITSCHKO SOLD HIS OLYMPIC MEDAL FOR $1 MILLION

## MEDAL FOR SALE

## (AND THE BUYER GAVE IT BACK)

## FACT OR FAKE?

The medal was auctioned in 2012 to raise funds for a charitable foundation set up by Wladimir and his brother to help children in their native Ukraine access sport and education.

## TELL ME MORE

Klitschko won his gold medal for super-heavyweight boxing at the 1996 Atlanta Olympics. In the same year he set up the Klitschko Foundation. Although the buyer won the medal, he immediately returned it to Klitschko, allowing him to keep it in the family.

**VERDICT**

**Fact**

12

# MICHAEL JORDAN
## WAS CUT FROM HIS HIGH SCHOOL BASKETBALL TEAM

## TELL ME MORE

Although even basketball legend Michael Jordan claims this to be true, the truth is a little more complicated. He tried out for the top high-school team, but was selected for a different one instead. He wasn't cut, because he was never selected.

Aged 15, Jordan tried out for his high school varsity team but wasn't selected. It was a real blow to Jordan as his best friend was selected. Instead, Jordan was selected for the junior varsity team. The 'cut' motivated Jordan to train harder and get better.

**VERDICT**
**Fake**

### DREAM TEAM
Michael Jordan was part of an all-star USA basketball team who took gold at the 1992 Olympics.

SWIMMER MICHAEL PHELPS HAS WON MORE OLYMPIC GOLD MEDALS THAN MANY COUNTRIES

US swimmer Michael Phelps won 23 gold medals in four Olympic games, a total that is beyond that of 66 countries, and way beyond the 44 countries who have no medals to their name.

## TELL ME MORE

Phelps first competed in the 2000 Olympics in Sydney at the age of just 15. At Athens in 2004 he took six golds and in Beijing 2008 he won every race he entered, taking home eight gold medals. In London 2012 he bagged another four golds and, instead of retiring, he went to Rio in 2016 for five more glorious golds!

## MORE MOST-MEDAL FACTS!

**COUNTRY:**
USA, 2,636 medals, 1,061 gold

**FEMALE ATHLETE:**
Larisa Latynina (Soviet gymnast), 18 medals, nine gold

**PARALYMPIAN:**
Trischa Zorn (US swimmer), 46 Paralympic medals, 32 gold

**VERDICT**
**Fact**

15

# ICE HOCKEY PUCKS MUST BE KEPT FROZEN

Brrrr ...

## FACT OR FAKE?

Pucks are made of rubber. The rubber has been through a process called vulcanisation to make it stronger, but even so, it's still bouncy. Freezing the pucks stops them being too bouncy.

## TELL ME MORE

Professional players really crack the puck around in this fast-paced sport, so the more they can control the puck the better and safer the play will be. Freezing the pucks means the players will be better able to control them. Pucks are constantly changed during the game, so a cooler full of frozen pucks is kept in the penalty box.

## PERFECT PUCKS

When ice hockey began in the 1800s, frozen dung, balls or blocks of wood were used for pucks.

## VERDICT
## Fact

I'm so hungry!

PP

# PIZZA-PAUL ATE PIZZAS WHILE CURLING

## FACT OR FAKE?

This is one of the great legends of curling: Pizza-Paul Gowsell ordered a pizza to arrive on the ice in the middle of a match.

VERDICT
Fake

## TELL ME MORE

Gowsell gained a reputation as a rebel within the sport of curling – he wore check trousers and generally had a good time. He explains that the pizza was necessary: the team were hungry *between* matches having unexpectedly reached the third-place playoff of a tournament. There was a long queue for food, so he ordered pizzas: 'a couple extra-large Specials, deluxe with everything on 'em. Except anchovies.'

# AMERICAN FOOTBALL GAMES TAKE OVER 3 HOURS

## FACT OR FAKE?

Officially, American football games have four 15-minute quarters, adding up to 60 minutes of game time. However, the clock is stopped so regularly that crowds are usually watching for more than three hours.

## TELL ME MORE

How is this possible, you ask? Well, there are lots of reasons for stopping the clock: half-time, reviews, injury, timeouts, and so on. American football is a game of set pieces: where the clock is stopped to reset the field and to change players. Other games, such as football and rugby, have free-flowing play with fewer reasons for stoppage.

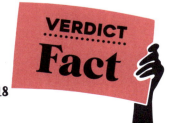

VERDICT
Fact

# THE TERM 'SOCCER' FOR FOOTBALL BEGAN IN AMERICA

## FACT OR FAKE?

What do you call the world's most popular sport? Some call it football, some call it soccer. Because 'soccer' is best known as the American term for football, most assume it started there.

### THE BEAUTIFUL GAME

It's not only the USA: Australia, Canada and New Zealand all use 'soccer'. Italians call football 'Calcio', Indonesians call it 'Sepak Bola' and Slovenia and Croatia call it 'nogomet'!

## TELL ME MORE

Rules for football were written down in England by the Football Association in 1863. It became known as 'association football', which was soon changed to 'soccer'. In the US, gridiron (now American) football had been invented, similar to both rugby and football. This became known as 'football' and association football as 'soccer'.

## VERDICT
## Fake

**19**

# RUGBY BALLS ARE

## EGG-SHAPED

## BECAUSE THEY WERE ONCE MADE WITH PIGS' BLADDERS

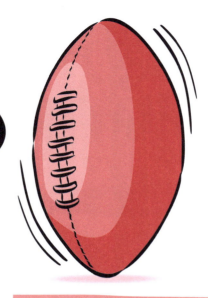

It's not known why rugby balls kept their distinctive oval, or egg shape. It may be because it is a ball-carrying game and an oval shape is easier to carry than a sphere. The official dimensions of the rugby ball were agreed in 1892 by the Rugby Football Union.

## FACT OR FAKE?

Before the invention of rubber, pigs' bladders were inflated and encased in leather to create a ball. Even when rubber was invented, the plum- or egg-like shape of the original balls was copied.

VERDICT
Fact

# WILLIAM WEBB ELLIS INVENTED RUGBY WHEN HE PICKED UP A FOOTBALL AND RAN WITH IT

Hey, come back!

## FACT OR FAKE?

This story has become so widely accepted that there is even a trophy named after him. However, the only account of the incident was written more than 50 years after it happened, by someone who wasn't there, and after Webb Ellis had passed away.

### CUP WINNERS
The Webb Ellis Cup is awarded to the winner of the Rugby World Cup!

VERDICT
**Fake**

## TELL ME MORE

The storyteller, Matthew Bloxam, claimed in a letter to a newspaper in 1876 that Webb Ellis had made his game-changing move in 1823. The incident was so long ago that the origins of the game are almost impossible to trace accurately. It may even have roots in an ancient Roman game!

# IT'S AGAINST THE RULES TO CATCH A BASEBALL IN YOUR MASK

## FACT OR FAKE?

It sounds unlikely, but there is a rule just in case a pitcher throws a ball that gets stuck in the grill of the catcher's mask (or any of their clothing). In this case any runners on bases can all move on one base.

## TELL ME MORE

The rule is number 5.06(c)(7): *A pitched ball lodges in the catcher's mask or paraphernalia, or in or against the umpire's body, mask or paraphernalia, and remains out of play, runners advance one base.* The umpire can increase the bases moved if they think the ball was hidden in clothing deliberately!

**VERDICT**
## Fact

22

Love you ...

# A FOOTBALL GOALIE CAN HOLD ON TO THE BALL FOR AS LONG AS THEY LIKE

## FACT OR FAKE?

This is one of those technical rules that referees can be quite lenient about. Most goalies want to keep the game moving so throw the ball quickly. However, rules state that they can hold the ball for only 6 seconds.

## TELL ME MORE

If a goalie fails to release the ball within 6 seconds the opposing team are awarded an indirect free kick. This rule was brought in to stop players deliberately wasting time, but as long as the referee can see that the goalie is actively looking to throw the ball they aren't too strict.

## VERDICT
....................
### Fake

### TAKE YOUR TIME
In 2015, Simon Mignolet held on to the ball for a whopping 22 seconds and gave away a free kick that led to a goal!

23

# A **70**-YEAR-OLD WOMAN RAN **7** MARATHONS IN **7** DAYS ON **7** CONTINENTS

## FACT OR FAKE?

Chau Smith took on this challenge, known as the Triple7Quest in 2017, to celebrate her 70th birthday. Chau lives in Kansas City, USA. She began running as a way to relax and soon took on the challenge of marathons.

## TELL ME MORE

Chau was born in Vietnam and lived through the Vietnam War (1954–75). At the age of 13, she was hit by shrapnel and still has pieces in her right leg and arm. She says she feels pain from them when running but has learned to cope with it.

VERDICT

**Fact**

# THE FIRST WOMAN TO CYCLE AROUND THE WORLD WAS A PROFESSIONAL ATHLETE

I'm definitely switching to men's clothes

## FACT OR FAKE?

Annie 'Londonderry' Kopchovsky wowed the world when, in 1884, she learnt to ride a bike and two days later set out on a round-the-world tour!

## TELL ME MORE

Annie was a working woman from Boston with three children under six when she took on the challenge to cycle the world. Plucky Annie got sponsorship by hanging a sign for Londonderry Spring Water on her bike and set off with a pearl pistol for protection. She completed the trip in 15 months and won $10,000.

### SHOCKING!

Not only did Annie cause a stir by setting off in the first place, but she also switched to men's clothes and a man's bike for most of her journey.

VERDICT

Fake

25

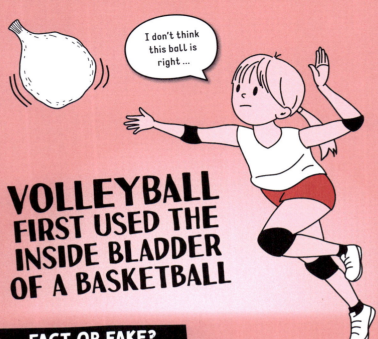

# VOLLEYBALL FIRST USED THE INSIDE BLADDER OF A BASKETBALL

## FACT OR FAKE?

Volleyball was originally played with basketballs, but they were too heavy. Following this, just the inside rubber bladder of the ball was used, but that was too light. At last, the company Spalding designed a ball that was just right. It should have been called 'goldilocks ball' ...

## TELL ME MORE

Volleyball was developed a few years after basketball (see page 10) by William Morgan. He saw how basketball had caught on, but could be too rough for older people. He combined badminton, tennis and basketball to create a non-contact sport called 'Mintonette' – later changed to volleyball.

**VERDICT**
Fact

# THE TOUR DE FRANCE LEADER WEARS A YELLOW JERSEY

## FACT OR FAKE?

The yellow jersey, or *maillot jaune*, is the most sought-after prize in the Tour de France as it is worn by the race leader. The colour yellow was chosen because it is easily visible.

## TELL ME MORE

When the Tour began, the leader would wear a green armband. As the Tour became more popular, with more spectators and reporters, people complained they could not see the leader. In 1919, the first official yellow jersey was given to the leader Eugène Christophe, to make him more visible.

## TOUR JERSEY PRIZES

YELLOW: the overall race winner, completing the race in the least time

GREEN: awarded to the rider with the most stage points

POLKA DOT: awarded to King of the Mountains (for the most mountain stage points)

VERDICT

Fact

# WINNING OVER 20 MARATHONS IS IMPOSSIBLE ...

## FACT OR FAKE?

Tatyana McFadden has had an incredible athletic career which began in Athens in 2004, when she made her Paralympic debut at the age of 15. She took two medals but was hungry for more ...

## TELL ME MORE

Tatyana initially competed in short distance wheelchair racing: 100 m, 200 m, 400 m; then moved on to longer distances, winning 23 major world marathons, and 17 Paralympic medals – seven of them gold. One of Tatyana's silver medals is for 2014 Winter Paralympics cross-country skiing!

### MAJOR MARATHONS

Tatyana has won four marathon Grand Slams (four major marathon titles in a year) in 2013, 2014, 2015 and 2016.

VERDICT
**Fake**

28

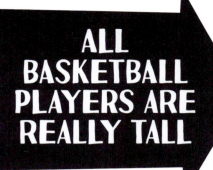

# ALL BASKETBALL PLAYERS ARE REALLY TALL

## FACT OR FAKE?

It's true, it helps to be tall in basketball, and the sport boasts some of the tallest athletes in the sporting world. However, there are some successful basketball players who come well under the 193 cm average.

## TELL ME MORE

Muggsy Bogues is probably the best known of the shorter basketball stars. He made his NBA debut in 1987 at 160 cm. Earl Boykins measured in at 165 cm and Spud Webb at 170 cm. What these players lacked in height they made up for in energy, skill and determination.

VERDICT

## Fake

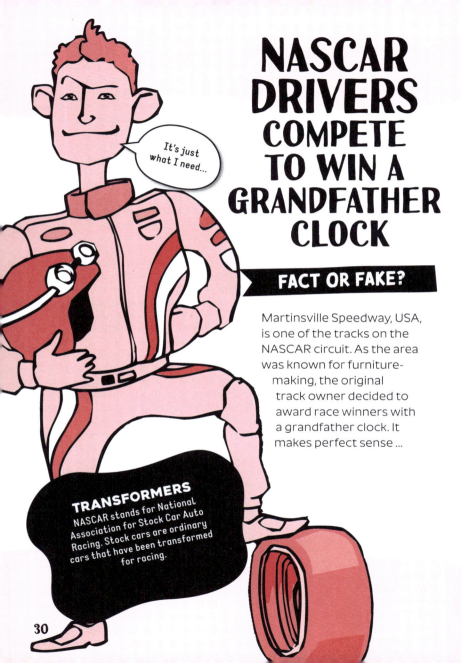

# NASCAR DRIVERS COMPETE TO WIN A GRANDFATHER CLOCK

It's just what I need...

## FACT OR FAKE?

Martinsville Speedway, USA, is one of the tracks on the NASCAR circuit. As the area was known for furniture-making, the original track owner decided to award race winners with a grandfather clock. It makes perfect sense ...

**TRANSFORMERS**

NASCAR stands for National Association for Stock Car Auto Racing. Stock cars are ordinary cars that have been transformed for racing.

## OTHER QUIRKY PRIZES

* ★ a live lobster,
  NASCAR racing
  (New Hampshire Speedway)
* ★ a green jacket,
  Masters golf
* ★ cheese,
  Italian Open golf
* ★ a cow or a reindeer,
  World Cup skiing
* ★ a granite cobblestone,
  Paris-Roubaix cycle race

## TELL ME MORE

First awarded in 1964, this towering trophy stands 2.13 m high. It's a sought-after prize in the sport and some drivers have even won more than one – retired driver Richard Petty has won 15!

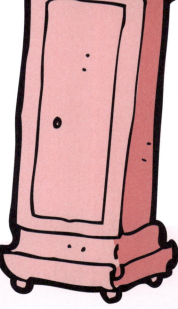

VERDICT
Fact

# FOOTBALL GOALKEEPERS CAN'T SCORE GOALS

## FACT OR FAKE?

You might think that being over 90 m away from the opposite goal would make it more or less impossible for keepers to score goals, but it happens, and probably more often than you think!

## TELL ME MORE

The record for the longest goal ever scored was from a goal kick: straight from goal to goal, covering a distance of over 96.01 m. At other times, teams looking for a late goal might call the goalie into the box to have the best possible chance of scoring, or a team might need their goalie to help out with penalty kicks.

**VERDICT**
.............
**Fake**

# ALL BASEBALLS HAVE 108 STITCHES

## FACT OR FAKE?

Baseballs are made from two figure-of-eight shaped pieces of leather. They are sewn together using 223 cm of waxed red thread. Red was chosen because it is more visible than blue or black.

## TELL ME MORE

Baseballs have been made in many ways over time. The first used melted shoe rubber for the core and, for a long time, pitchers had to make their own balls. Baseballs were standardised for competition play in the 1850s and 108 was found to be the perfect number of stitches!

## WHAT'S INSIDE?

The inside of a baseball is made of cork, surrounded by rubber, wound up in yarn and covered in cowhide.

### VERDICT
**Fact**

33

# PLAYING VIDEO GAMES DOESN'T COUNT AS SPORT

Sports require: competitions; physical attributes such as athleticism, stamina, quick responses and coordination; fans and spectators; and players dedicated to training and improving. None of these things happen in video gaming, or do they?

## TELL ME MORE

Many argue that electronic sports, or e-sports, share the characteristics of sport listed here. The video game industry is huge, international and diverse. Competitions can take place in big arenas with commentators and spectators; players participate in teams or individually; top players are well-paid in prize money and sponsorship ... It sounds like a sport to me!

VERDICT
Fake

# LANGUR MONKEYS WERE PART OF THE

## SECURITY TEAM

## AT THE 2010 COMMONWEALTH GAMES

Settle down!

## FACT OR FAKE?

When the Commonwealth Games were held in Delhi, India, in 2010, the police used trained langur monkeys to help keep other monkeys away from the venues. The boxing and hockey venues were of particular concern to officials.

## TELL ME MORE

Many thousands of monkeys roam freely in Indian cities as they are a protected species, but they do cause problems. Langur monkeys were trained for use by the police in controlling them, until 2012 when it was banned by the government.

VERDICT
## Fact

## FISHY STORY

At the Delhi games, special fish were put into a pond in the centre of the complex. It was hoped that they would eat the larvae of mosquitoes, to stop adult mosquitoes bothering athletes and spectators.

# THERE IS A PINEAPPLE ON TOP OF THE WIMBLEDON TROPHY BECAUSE THAT'S WHAT THE WINNER ONCE WON!

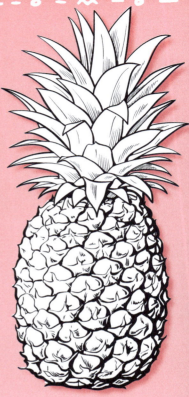

## FACT OR FAKE?

The pineapple-topped trophy was first presented in 1887, but no one seems to know exactly why this exotic fruit was chosen for the top. Rather than pineapples, winners received a replica trophy and prize money.

## TELL ME MORE

The pineapple trophy is still used today, but an extra stand has been added below to make space for more winners' names to be added. The most likely reason for the pineapple on top is that it was a luxury item in the 1800s and so was a symbol of wealth.

VERDICT
Fake

# THE FIRST EVER WINNER OF THE TOUR DE FRANCE WAS LATER DISQUALIFIED FOR TAKING THE TRAIN

## FACT OR FAKE?

The first Tour de France took place in 1903. Italian Maurice Garin won easily over his competitors. Garin entered for a second year, in 1904, and apparently jumped on a train to shorten a tricky stage.

## TELL ME MORE

Following the 1904 race, the organisers stripped the four top riders of their titles. No records are left of their investigations. Today, only tales remain of Garin as an old man admitting to hopping on a train.

## CALM DOWN!

The first Tour caught the public eye and the second year was hugely popular. However, fans went totally over the top, sabotaging and even attacking other entrants to help out their favourites.

## VERDICT
# Fact

# THE LONGEST EVER BOXING MATCH LASTED 110 ROUNDS AND TOOK 7 HOURS

## FACT OR FAKE?

In 1893 two boxers, Andy Bowen and Jack Burke, stepped into the ring in New Orleans, Louisiana, USA, for what was supposed to be an ordinary fight. They left 110 rounds and over 7 hours later ... in a draw.

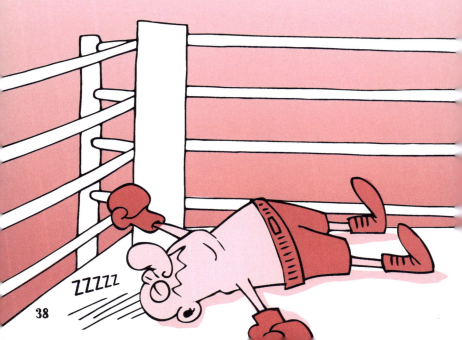

ZZZZZ

The contest was for the Lightweight Champion of the South. Burke won the first 25 rounds, was then knocked down in the 25th, but the bell rang before he was counted out. Eventually, by the 110th round, both were too exhausted to continue and the referee called it a draw.

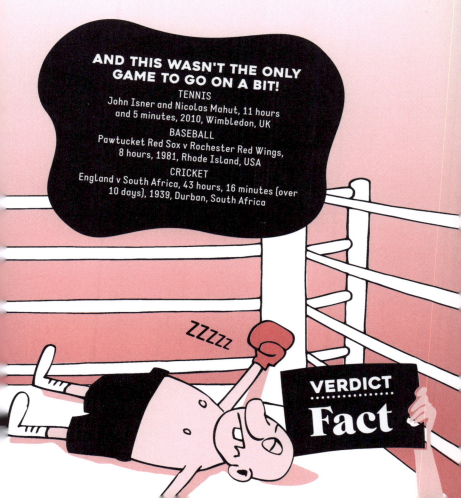

**AND THIS WASN'T THE ONLY GAME TO GO ON A BIT!**

TENNIS
John Isner and Nicolas Mahut, 11 hours and 5 minutes, 2010, Wimbledon, UK

BASEBALL
Pawtucket Red Sox v Rochester Red Wings, 8 hours, 1981, Rhode Island, USA

CRICKET
England v South Africa, 43 hours, 16 minutes (over 10 days), 1939, Durban, South Africa

ZZZzzz

**VERDICT**

*Fact*

# YOU CAN'T PLAY SPORT IN SPACE

## FACT OR FAKE?

Not only do some astronauts going to the International Space Station (ISS) take frisbees and boomerangs with them, but one member of the Apollo 14 crew decided to play golf on the Moon!

## TELL ME MORE

As there is no gravity in space, exercise is really important to keep your bones and muscles strong. Sport is a good way of keeping exercise fun! Some astronauts set up relay races or invent new games. In 2007, Sunita Williams ran the Boston Marathon on a treadmill on the ISS. After running for 90 minutes, she had also completed a full orbit of the Earth.

### SPACE BALLS!
The golf ball that Apollo 14 astronaut Alan Shepard Jr. hit on the Moon, is still there.

VERDICT
............
Fake

# SOME SWIMSUITS HAVE BEEN BANNED FOR MAKING SWIMMERS *FASTER*

In 2009 at the swimming World Championships in Rome, 43 world records were broken. They have been nicknamed the 'Plastic Games' as so many swimmers were wearing high-tech suits that improved their performance.

## TELL ME MORE

FINA, the governing body for world swimming, found the new suits gave wearers too much of an advantage. The suits were made of water-repelling polyurethane plastic, rather than a woven textile. As well as banning the material polyurethane, FINA also changed the regulations to ban full-body suits.

I feel under-dressed!

**VERDICT**

## Fact

# MARTINA HINGIS BECAME WORLD NUMBER ONE AT

## AGE 16

## FACT OR FAKE?

Martina Hingis became world tennis number one in 1996 when she won the ladies' singles Australian Open, Wimbledon and the US Open. She was 16 years old. In 1998 she took the Australian Open title again and was number one in both ladies' singles and doubles.

## TELL ME MORE

Martina's mother was a professional tennis player and coached her from a young age. At the age of 12, Martina won the junior French Open, then at the age of 13 she won the Junior Wimbledon title. At the age of 15 she won the Wimbledon ladies' doubles with her partner, Helen Sukova.

**VERDICT**

**Fact**

# YOU CAN'T PLAY SPORT UNDER WATER

## FACT OR FAKE?

Sport is one of those things that people will try no matter where they are! Whether on the Moon (see page 40), under the sea or just about anywhere, you can bet that someone has played sport there. Although it might seem impossible, many sports have been tried under water!

## TELL ME MORE

Sports such as free diving, finswimming and aquathlon are underwater activities that have been made into sports. Other underwater sports are land sports that people play under water, including football, hockey, rugby, boxing and even … ice hockey!

## NOW THAT'S COLD

Underwater ice hockey is an extreme sport played under a 6 m by 8 m frozen rink or pond. Players don't have breathing equipment. Instead, they surface for air every 30 seconds!

VERDICT
**Fake**

43

# IRONMAN COMPETITIONS WERE ORIGINALLY CREATED FOR ROBOTS

## FACT OR FAKE?

The first IRONMAN event was held in Hawaii on 18 February 1978. It was the dream of John and Judy Collins who loved triathlons and set up the race around the island, a mammoth course of 226 km.

## TELL ME MORE

The first race had 15 participants. After that its popularity grew and in 1980 the Collinses gave the ABC television company permission to film the event, creating a global audience. Today, there are more than 170 IRONMAN triathlons held worldwide.

## THE IRON COWBOY
In 2015, James Lawrence completed 50 IRONMAN triathlons, in 50 days, in 50 different US states!

VERDICT
Fake

# TENNIS GRUNTS ARE LINKED TO ANCIENT WAR CRIES!

## FACT OR FAKE?

Each tennis season the debate over whether some players' vocalisations are too noisy begins again. Despite some of the cries being quite fearsome, there is no evidence of them being linked to ancient war cries.

## TELL ME MORE

Some players are taught to grunt as they hit the ball: making a sound helps them to breathe out sharply, which helps to stabilise the shot. However, some players have reached such decibels that their opponents claim they cannot hear the ball being struck, and so are disadvantaged.

## VERDICT
### Fake

45

# SHEEP COUNT

## FACT OR FAKE?

Along with Aussie Rules, rugby, netball and cricket, sheep counting is a sport that Australians just love – well, some of them.

## TELL ME MORE

Held for the first time in 2006, sheep counting contests consist of letting a lot of sheep go and, you guessed it, counting them. The winner is the one who gets closest to the actual total.

## OTHER UNLIKELY SPORTS

★ worm charming (see page 58)
★ cheese rolling
★ wife-carrying
★ bog snorkelling
★ extreme ironing
★ toe wrestling

VERDICT

**Fact**

# THE FASTEST ICE HOCKEY HAT-TRICK TOOK JUST 21 SECONDS

## FACT OR FAKE?

In March 1952, the New York Rangers played the Chicago Black Hawks at Madison Square Garden, New York, USA. The Chicago captain, Bill Mosienko, made hat-trick history!

## TELL ME MORE

The Chicago Hawks were down 6-2 in the last quarter of the game. Then the magic happened: at 6.09, 6.20 and 6.30 Mosienko scored goals. In just 21 seconds he took the score to 6-5. He missed another goal 45 seconds after this, but a teammate managed to score twice more to win the game 7-6.

## VERDICT
### Fact

# 13 IS TOO YOUNG TO WIN A GOLD MEDAL

## FACT OR FAKE?

In 2008, Ellie Simmonds won two gold medals for swimming in the Paralympic Games. She was 13 at the time. The following year she won six gold medals at the Swimming World Championships Short Course. In 2010, she took four golds at the Swimming World Championships.

## TELL ME MORE

Ellie's success continued in 2012 at the London Olympics where she took two more golds and broke two world records. In total she has nine gold medals. Ellie started swimming at the age of five and was inspired to aim for Paralympic glory when she watched the 2004 games in Athens.

## VERDICT
## Fake

### YOUNG WINNERS

AGE 13: Momiji Nishiya, 2021, Olympic gold in street skateboarding

AGE 12: Jessica Long, 2004, 3 gold medals, paralympic swimming

# LAURA DEKKER SAILED AROUND THE WORLD SOLO AGED JUST 14

Laura Dekker was determined to take the trip of her life! She worked hard and at age 14, she set off to sail around the world single-handedly.

Laura set off alone from Gibraltar in August 2010. First, she sailed to the Canary Islands, then west across the North Atlantic, through the Panama Canal, across the Pacific, through the Torres Strait, around the Cape of Good Hope and across the South Atlantic to the Caribbean. She finished her epic voyage at Sint Maarten in January 2012.

VERDICT

Fact

# BEFORE THE PARALYMPICS, ATHLETES WITH DISABILITIES COULD NOT COMPETE

## FACT OR FAKE?

In 1904, George Eyser competed in the gymnastics events of the Olympic games. He took three gold medals, two silver and a bronze, and he competed with a wooden leg.

## TELL ME MORE

George lived in Saint Louis, Missouri, USA. His family had emigrated from Germany in 1884. Eyser lost part of his left leg in a childhood injury and wore a prosthetic limb that attached above the knee, made partly of wood. Eyser took gold in the parallel bars, the 25-foot rope climb and the vault.

## VERDICT
·············
## Fake

### FIRST GAMES
It wasn't until 1960 that the first Paralympic games took place in Rome, Italy.

# THE CRICKET
## CONTAINS

## FACT OR FAKE?

The original Ashes urn was tiny, about 15 cm tall, and apparently contained a burnt set of bails (wooden pieces that balance on top of the stumps). Although it gave the contest its name, it was never used as the official trophy.

TWHACK!

**VERDICT**
........................
## Fake

# ASHES TROPHY
# REAL ASHES

In 1882, England lost to Australia at the Oval cricket ground in London, UK. The *Sporting Times* newspaper printed a joke notice of the death of English cricket (see right). When they later won in Australia, England were presented with a tiny urn containing ashes.

Today, the Ashes series is five test matches between the English and Australian cricket teams, held about every two years. The winners get a crystal glass trophy.

## ASHES OBITUARY

In Affectionate Remembrance of English Cricket which died at the Oval on 29th August 1882.

Deeply lamented by a large circle of sorrowing friends and acquaintances.

## RIP

N.B. The body will be cremated and the ashes taken to Australia.

# A MARATHON IS THE EXACT DISTANCE THAT MESSENGER PHEIDIPPIDES RAN IN 490 BCE

## FACT OR FAKE?

In 490 BCE, Pheidippides, a running messenger for the Greek army, was sent from the battlefield of Marathon back to Athens, to announce a great victory of the Greek army over the Persians.

## TELL ME MORE

The marathon event created for the first modern Olympics was named after this incredible journey, which was just under 40 km. Today's marathon distance of 42.195 km was set at the 1908 London Olympics. It was just over 41 km from Windsor Castle to the Olympic Stadium; adding another 352 m loop allowed King Edward to watch from inside the castle!

## IT'S MY JOB

Pheidippides was a *hemereodromos* – a day runner or courier in the Greek military. It was his job to deliver messages, on foot, over huge distances.

## VERDICT
........
# Fake

# THE FASTEST BADMINTON IS OVER 490 KPH!

In 2013, Malaysian Tan Boon Heong attempted to beat the world record for the fastest badminton hit (not in a game), which stood at 421 kph. He smashed it, literally, with a new record of 493 kph!

## TELL ME MORE

Of all the shots in badminton, the smash reaches the fastest speeds. The record for the fastest smash during a game stands at 426 kph and was achieved by Mads Pieler Kolding of Denmark in 2017. It's not only the smashes that are speedy: in 1996 Ra Kyung-min of South Korea beat England's Julia Mann in a match that lasted just 6 minutes!

VERDICT
Fact

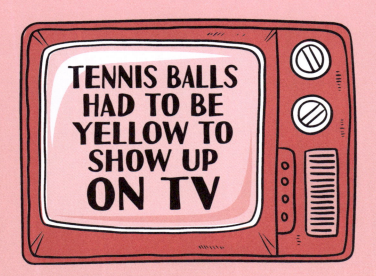

# TENNIS BALLS HAD TO BE YELLOW TO SHOW UP ON TV

## FACT OR FAKE?

Tennis was first shown on colour television in the 1970s. The International Tennis Federation (ITF) introduced yellow balls in 1972 as research found they were more visible on screen.

## TELL ME MORE

Before 1972, the balls used were black or white. Screen trials were carried out to see which colour would be best and 'optic yellow' was chosen. Tennis tournament Wimbledon continued to use black or white balls until 1986.

### ROYAL TENNIS

In his play *Henry V*, Shakespeare shows young King Henry being given tennis balls by the French prince. In reply, he says:

*When we have march'd our rackets to these balls,*

*We will, in France, by God's grace, play a set*

## VERDICT
## Fact

Coming through!

# THE MODERN PENTATHLON WAS INSPIRED BY A SOLDIER DELIVERING A MESSAGE

## FACT OR FAKE?

Modern Olympics founder Baron de Coubertin created the modern pentathlon as a contest for the complete athlete – a test of strength, fitness and skill. It is said that he was inspired by the life of a cavalry officer.

## TELL ME MORE

The story goes that a cavalry officer once had to swordfight, swim, run and fire shots all to deliver a message. It is said that De Coubertin used this example to create a new version of the pentathlon that featured in the ancient Olympic games. Then contestants would run, jump, wrestle and throw the discus and spear.

## VERDICT
# Fact

You guys are amazing – handsome too!

Too kind!

# WORM CHARMING IS AN ACTUAL SPORT!

## FACT OR FAKE?

The aim of worm charming is to bring as many worms to the surface as possible. Contestants can use any means to charm worms: tinging forks, tapping the ground and sprinkling any liquid (as long as they are willing to drink it first!).

## TELL ME MORE

At the time of writing, the record for most worms charmed in 15 minutes is held by Sophie Smith who managed to charm 567 worms to the surface of a 3 m square plot. She set the record in 2009 at the age of 10!

### GRUNTING

In the USA, worm charming may also be known as worm grunting, a tradition that comes from collecting worms for fishing bait.

## VERDICT
## Fact

# THE SWISS GUARDS AND THE MUSEUM GUARDS PLAY FOR THE VATICAN CITY FOOTBALL TEAM

## FACT OR FAKE?

Vatican City state is home to around 800 people, yet it still boasts a thriving football scene. Teams are made up of the departments of the Holy See – the governing organisation of the Roman Catholic Church.

## TELL ME MORE

Today, Vatican City has national men's and women's teams, but is not part of FIFA. It runs leagues and competitions, and teams play against other non-FIFA countries such as Monaco. The most popular competition is the Clericus Cup which sees students compete for the glory of a trophy blessed by the Pope himself.

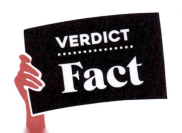

VERDICT
## Fact

# BEING AN ATHLETE IS A FULL-TIME JOB

## FACT OR FAKE?

Although training for top sports takes a lot of time and commitment, many sports don't make enough money to pay athletes, so they have to have day jobs too.

## TELL ME MORE

Athletes competing in the Olympics often have full-time jobs: American Gwen Jorgensen is a gold medal triathlete and qualified accountant; American bronze-medal fencer Race Imboden is also a DJ. Norwegian Olaf Tufte has won two gold medals, one silver and one bronze in rowing, while also being a fireman and a farmer!

VERDICT
Fake

# RACEHORSE NAMES CANNOT BE MORE THAN 18 CHARACTERS LONG

## FACT OR FAKE?

While you can get really creative with racehorse names, there are some rules to follow: the 18 characters includes spaces, no punctuation is allowed other than apostrophes and you cannot have more than seven syllables.

## TELL ME MORE

The other rules for racehorse names relate to the content: you cannot have anything rude or offensive, anyone's name unless they have agreed it with you, a famous horse's name or any websites.

### VERDICT
Fact

### SAVED BY THE SEA

As a foal, famous racehorse Red Rum had bone disease in his foot. His trainer ran him on the sand and shallow sea, and Red Rum went on to win the Grand National race three times!

# NETBALL IS JUST FOR GIRLS

## FACT OR FAKE?

No sport should be only for girls or boys. Although netball started as a women's alternative to basketball, today both men and women play it all over the world.

## TELL ME MORE

Netball was originally developed from basketball. Some say the difference came from a misunderstanding of the rules, others that changing the play allowed for women's more restrictive clothing. In Australia and New Zealand, it was known as 'women's basketball' until around 1970.

### NET BALL

The name netball comes from the posts: they were changed from basketball's hoops with backboards, to netted hoops on a post.

**VERDICT**
.............
**Fake**

# REAL TENNIS BALLS WERE MADE FROM HUMAN HAIR

## FACT OR FAKE?

Real tennis was one of the games that developed into tennis as we know it today. The balls were made by stuffing a sphere of material with rags, horsehair, animal intestines or even human hair!

## TELL ME MORE

Real tennis began in the 1400s. It was also called Royal Tennis or the Sport of Kings. It was played indoors and the ball didn't bounce.

In the 1920s Westminster Hall in London was restored and during the works, balls were found in the roof that were made from putty and human hair!

**VERDICT**

**Fact**

# QUIDDITCH IS NOW A REAL SPORT

**FACT OR FAKE?**

Fans of J.K. Rowling's *Harry Potter* books are keen to make this fictitious game a reality. Undeterred by not being able to fly, there are now leagues of muggles competing in quidditch competitions all over the world.

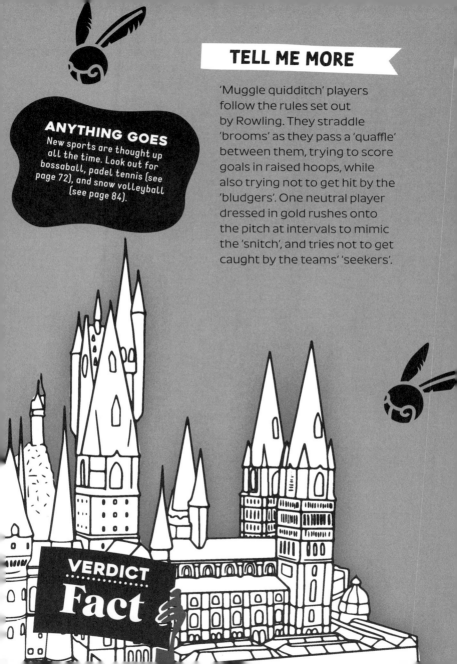

## TELL ME MORE

'Muggle quidditch' players follow the rules set out by Rowling. They straddle 'brooms' as they pass a 'quaffle' between them, trying to score goals in raised hoops, while also trying not to get hit by the 'bludgers'. One neutral player dressed in gold rushes onto the pitch at intervals to mimic the 'snitch', and tries not to get caught by the teams' 'seekers'.

### ANYTHING GOES
New sports are thought up all the time. Look out for bossaball, padel tennis (see page 72), and snow volleyball (see page 84).

**VERDICT**
**Fact**

# SUMO WRESTLERS ARE UNHEALTHY

## FACT OR FAKE?

Sumo wrestlers are known for their size. Some can weigh in at 180 kg and eat as much as 7,000 calories a day. But sumo wrestlers are athletes with intense training programmes and carefully planned diets.

## TELL ME MORE

Sumo wrestling is all about mass. The more mass something has, the harder it is to move. Great news for sumo wrestlers who lose points by stepping or being forced out of the ring. Sumo wrestlers train hard every day to gain muscle and keep fat to just under their skin, rather than around vital organs.

### SUMO STABLE

The training camps that Japanese sumo wrestlers live in are called stables. Every competitor's hair is shaped in the same way for competition – the shape represents a ginkgo tree leaf.

### VERDICT
## Fake

# THE 1912 OLYMPICS INCLUDED AN ARTS COMPETITION

In 1912 an announcement was made that the Olympics that year would feature a 'Concours d'Art': an Art Competition. Baron de Coubertin entered the literature category and took gold!

## TELL ME MORE

Baron de Coubertin was the founder of the modern Olympics. The art competition included categories for architecture, sculpture, painting, music and literature. All works had to celebrate sport. De Coubertin's piece was called 'Ode to Sport' and was entered in both French and German languages, under the names Georges Hohrod and M. Eschbach.

**VERDICT**
**Fact**

67

# HAWK-EYE TECHNOLOGY IS NAMED AFTER RUFUS THE HAWK

Rufus the Hawk is the Harris hawk used by the Wimbledon tennis tournament to keep pigeons away from the tennis courts. Despite sharing this elegant raptor's keen vision, the tennis technology is actually named after someone else.

## TELL ME MORE

Hawk-Eye technology accurately tracks the movement of the ball, allowing officials to check exactly where it has travelled and bounced. This tech is now used by many sports including tennis, cricket, football, rugby, baseball ... the list goes on! It is named after the inventor, Paul Hawkins.

**VERDICT**
.............
## Fake

# RUNNER ABEBE BIKILA WON AN OLYMPIC MARATHON BAREFOOT

## FACT OR FAKE?

At the age of 28, Ethiopian Abebe Bikila travelled to Rome for the 1960 Olympic Games. He entered the marathon and ran the race barefoot as he always did. One kilometre before the line, he made his break and won by 200 m.

## TELL ME MORE

Bikala and his coach, Onni Niskanen, decided he should make the break at the site of the obelisk of Axun, which happened to be 1 km before the finish. The obelisk was in fact an Ethiopian monument that had been taken by Italian troops years before.

### RECORD BREAKER

Bikila returned to compete in the 1964 Tokyo Olympics. He won by a full four minutes, this time wearing socks and shoes. He set a world record despite having surgery on his appendix a month before!

VERDICT

Fact

# CRICKET UMPIRES HAVE TO IGNORE PLAYER APPEALS

## FACT OR FAKE?

In a bizarre cricket law, the umpire may not call a player out, even if they are out, unless he receives an appeal from a fielder. So that explains why the fielders call out to the umpire at each opportunity!

## TELL ME MORE

Fielders need to appeal before the ball is bowled again. A general cricketing term 'How's that?' can be used by fielders to appeal any sort of 'out' – being bowled, caught, leg before wicket, run out or stumped!

### SPOOKY STATS

When he retired, English cricketer Alec Stewart had scored 8,463 runs. In a spooky coincidence his date of birth is 8th April 1963: 8.4.63.

### VERDICT
## Fake

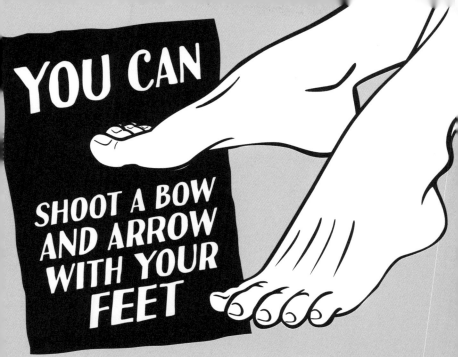

# YOU CAN

## SHOOT A BOW AND ARROW WITH YOUR FEET

Well, Brittany Walsh can! Using her feet, Brittany shot an arrow 12.31 m to set the world record in 2018. The incredible thing about this record is that she was also balancing on her hands!

## TELL ME MORE

Not only is Brittany an excellent gymnast, she's also an incredible archer. She combines both skills to demonstrate mind-blowing exploits all over the world. She trained and competed in gymnastics from a young age before joining a physical theatre company. She can perform her acrobatic archery blindfolded and with flaming arrows!

**VERDICT**
**Fact**

# PADEL TENNIS IS PLAYED IN THE WATER

## FACT OR FAKE?

Padel tennis is an exciting sport played on land and first developed in Mexico. It's a cross between tennis and squash and is the second most popular sport in Spain.

## TELL ME MORE

Football star Lionel Messi has his own padel court, and tennis brothers Andy and Jamie Murray, and footie coach Jürgen Klopp are fans. Padel tennis is played in doubles. The court is smaller than a tennis court and has clear-glass walls that the ball is allowed to bounce off.

### IN A PICKLE

Another form of tennis is pickleball. It's a mix of tennis, table tennis and badminton. Players use a solid bat and a plastic ball with holes in.

## VERDICT

**Fake**

# BOXERS NEED TO EAT LOTS OF RAW EGGS

Guzzling down raw eggs as part of a boxing diet was made famous by Sylvester Stallone in the *Rocky* boxing films. However, this really isn't essential to the sport.

## TELL ME MORE

Eggs are a fantastic source of protein and are, therefore, recommended, along with other protein-rich foods, for many boxers' diets. Protein helps muscles to repair and grow. The egg white is mainly water and protein, and the yolk contains lots of other nutrients as well.

**VERDICT**
## Fake

# OVER 8,000 PEOPLE
## TOOK PART IN THE WORLD'S LARGEST TAEKWONDO DISPLAY

## FACT OR FAKE?

On 21 April 2018, 8,212 people gathered for the largest ever taekwondo display. It took place in Korea with the intention of spreading a peaceful message ahead of an inter-Korean summit.

## TELL ME MORE

The incredible display was held in Seoul, South Korea. Participants of all ages wore traditional taekwondo uniforms and performed a synchronised 10-minute routine. Taekwondo is an ancient Korean martial art that includes kicks, blocks and punches brought together in *poomsae* – patterns or sequences.

VERDICT
Fact

# MUHAMMAD ALI

## THREW HIS GOLD MEDAL IN THE OHIO RIVER

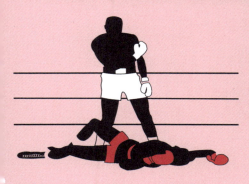

## FACT OR FAKE?

This story is a bit of a mystery: Muhammad Ali himself told an interviewer that he had thrown the medal into the river, then said he'd actually just misplaced it. Then someone claimed to have found it in the Ohio River!

## TELL ME MORE

Ali won his gold medal at the 1960 Rome Olympics and wore it proudly. Then, after a racist incident where he was refused service in a restaurant, he claimed to have thrown the medal in the river. Later he told reporters he had lost it. Then in 2012, an Ohio resident helping with a river cleaning project apparently found a medal from the 1960 Rome games …

### THE GREATEST

When Muhammad Ali retired in 1981 he had won 56 of his 61 fights. He won the world heavyweight title in 1964 and defended this title 19 times!

## VERDICT

Who knows!

75

# FREESTYLE SKIING
## WAS ALSO KNOWN AS
# 'HOTDOGGING'

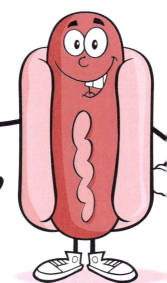

Rule-heavy alpine skiing was too strict for some skiers of the 1960s, so with jumps, flips and spins they started rewriting the rulebook. Nicknamed 'Hotdog skiing' this crazy sport was the new cool!

As early as the 1920s people had tried being more experimental with skiing, but hotdogging really took off in the 1960s. Hotdogs had been around in the USA since the 1890s. It's hard to know what links them to freestyle skiing … Perhaps it's because they are linked with relaxed eating, in contrast to formal dining?

### FREESTYLE STYLE

There are now 13 separate events in Olympic freestyle skiing. The most recent addition is BIG AIR, where skiers launch off a ramp and perform tricks in the air before landing.

VERDICT
**Fact**

# BAD WEATHER MEANS NO PLAY

## FACT OR FAKE?

Although at school we might all wish for sports matches to be cancelled in bad weather, they rarely are. Driving wind, rain, fog, ice and snow are all conditions teams must prepare to play in.

**VERDICT**
............
**Fake**

## TELL ME MORE

No match was colder than the 1967 NFL 'Ice Bowl'. American football teams the Green Bay Packers played the Dallas Cowboys in -25°C, with a wind chill of -44°C. In 1975, after heavy rain, the All Blacks rugby team played Scotland on a flooded pitch. Rain does, however, stop play in cricket. Constantly.

# THE WHITE HOUSE HAS ITS OWN BOWLING ALLEY

Strike!

## FACT OR FAKE?

You might think the President of the United States wouldn't have much time to relax. But when he or she does, the White House is well kitted out for this busy bod to kick back ...

## TELL ME MORE

The White House bowling alley was built in 1947 and opened by President Truman. In 1950, the White House staff formed their own bowling team. Presidents Johnson and Nixon both installed new lanes. President Clinton and First Lady Melania Trump both renovated the bowling alley during their time in the White House.

## ALL THE SPORTS

As well as a bowling alley, the White House has tennis courts, a swimming pool, a games room for billiards and table tennis, a jogging track and a putting green.

VERDICT
*Fact*

Such fun!

# SPLASHING IN WATER POLO IS ALL PART OF THE FUN

## FACT OR FAKE?

Watching water polo, it might seem as if everyone is splashing about. But *deliberate* splashing to the face is counted as a major foul and will see players sent out of the pool for 20 seconds.

## TELL ME MORE

Given that you are not allowed to touch the bottom of the pool in water polo, a certain amount of splashing is necessary as you swim about and compete for the ball. As well as the no face splashing rule, players are not allowed to take the ball under the water or grab it with two hands (apart from the goalie).

VERDICT

**Fake**

## THE FIRST EVER OLYMPIC MASCOT WAS A ...

# DACHSHUND

### FACT OR FAKE?

Waldi the dachshund was created for the Olympic Games in Munich 1972. He was the first ever Olympic mascot and was designed at a Christmas party.

### TELL ME MORE

At the organising committee's Christmas party, crayons, paper and modelling clay were given out so that partygoers could create mascot designs! Dachshunds are popular animals in Germany and Waldi was supposed to represent endurance, tenacity and agility.

### VERDICT
# Fact

# YOU HAVE TO BE QUIET AT TENNIS MATCHES

It is definitely expected that the crowd fall silent at tennis matches and players often wait for quiet before taking their shot. But it's not actually in the rule book ...

## TELL ME MORE

Some believe that history is to blame, as it was once a sport watched and played by the upper classes who required a level of quiet decorum, restrained enthusiasm and good behaviour. Players argue that in high-level tennis, they can hear the way a shot has been played by their opponent and that quiet is needed for concentration.

### HOORAY!
Quiet sports might be missing out! Studies have shown that crowds cheering at matches may affect the play, giving the home team an advantage!

VERDICT
**Fake**

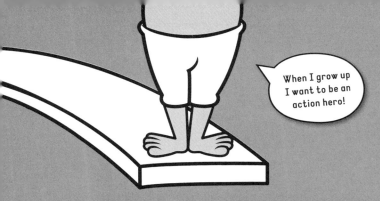

When I grow up I want to be an action hero!

# ACTOR JASON STATHAM WAS PART OF THE BRITISH NATIONAL DIVING SQUAD

## FACT OR FAKE?

Although he's best known for playing tough action heroes, Jason Statham had a career in diving before moving to the silver screen.

## TELL ME MORE

Statham began diving at a young age and made it on to the British National Diving Squad. He competed at the 1990 Commonwealth Games and the 1992 World Championships. Next, he tried modelling, before launching into movie stardom.

### TRUCK DIVE

Jason Statham put his swimming and diving skills to use on the set of *Expendables 3* when a stunt went wrong. He was driving a truck when the brakes failed and it plunged into the sea!

VERDICT

*Fact*

# WHEELCHAIR BASKETBALL IS A TOTALLY DIFFERENT GAME FROM BASKETBALL

## FACT OR FAKE?

Wheelchair basketball was developed in the 1940s as a way of helping soldiers injured in the Second World War (1939–45) to recover. The first competitions were between six US Army hospitals. The game's popularity spread around the world.

## TELL ME MORE

While a few of the rules have been adapted for the game to work for wheelchairs, the majority of the rules are the same as the original ones. The scoring system, the court, hoops and ball are all the same, too.

**VERDICT**
········
## Fake

# YOU CAN PLAY VOLLEYBALL IN THE SNOW

Beach and indoor volleyball are the best-known forms of the game. But, not wanting to miss an opportunity to play in the winter, some seriously cool volleyballers have started playing in the snow too.

## TELL ME MORE

Snow volleyball is very similar to beach or indoor games. Two teams of three face each other over a high net. The snow must be compacted and 30 cm deep. Players wear thermal clothing under their usual kit, and football boots to stop them slipping.

### JUMP! JUMP!
On average, a volleyball player will jump 300 times in each game!

## VERDICT
## Fact

84

# SKATEBOARDING BEGAN LIFE AS 'SIDEWALK SURFING'

## TELL ME MORE

The first competitions were held in the 1960s but skateboarding was quite dangerous as then the wheels used were made of clay – which could break easily. In the 1970s hard plastic wheels were invented and sidewalk surfing became properly established. Tricks were invented, then vert ramps appeared. In 1995 the first X Games competition was held, showcasing the sport for the masses.

## FACT OR FAKE?

Skateboarding began in the 1950s. Surfers, more used to riding waves, stuck roller skate wheels to the bottom of wooden boards and tried out their moves on the streets.

**VERDICT**

## Fact

# ATHLETES EAT AN ENORMOUS AMOUNT OF CALORIES

## FACT OR FAKE?

Marathon runners load up on pasta, boxers go crazy for eggs, rugby players eat anything and everything – these are all myths.

## TELL ME MORE

In reality, each athlete has their own needs and their diet depends on their training routine at the time. On average, men need around 2,500 calories a day and women need 2,000 calories. An athlete training for a big competition might need two or three times this. It all depends who you are and what you are doing.

VERDICT
............
Fake

# SNURFING IS A POPULAR WINTER SPORT

## FACT OR FAKE?

Head up the slopes with your fellow snurfers and come snurfing down. Sherman Poppen is credited with inventing the snow-surfer in 1965 and his wife came up with the term 'snurfing'.

## TELL ME MORE

The board that Poppen went on to launch as a product was flat and straight with a rise at the front. There was a rope attached to the front for the rider to hold on to. Poppen's original design was modified as the trend caught on and became the popular sport known as snowboarding today!

## IT'S MY MOUNTAIN

When snowboarding first became popular, traditional skiers didn't want the newbies on 'their' mountains and snowboarders were excluded!

### VERDICT
## Fact

# FRISBEE WAS INVENTED BY STUDENTS THROWING PIE DISHES

Look out!

## FACT OR FAKE?

The inventor of the frisbee, Fred Morrison, first used a popcorn container lid to fling back and forth, and then a cake tin. His wife also loved the pastime and soon they came up with a rubber toy version.

## TELL ME MORE

Fred experimented with names: the Flying Cake Pan, Whirlo-Way, Flying Saucer, Pluto Platter, but none of them really stuck. He sold the toy to the Wham-O toy company. They named it the 'frisbee' after the Frisbie Pie company, because people liked to whirl their dishes about too!

### NO FRISBEE FOR ME!
Inventor Fred Morrison hated the name 'frisbee' and thought it would never 'fly'!

VERDICT
**Fake**

# THE US NAVY TRIED TO USE FRISBEES TO LAUNCH FLARES

## FACT OR FAKE?

This project was described in a 1972 newspaper as a 'frisbee fiasco'. In 1968, the US Navy spent $375,000 testing a frisbee-flare, but sadly it was a flop!

## TELL ME MORE

A frisbee stays in the air for a long time once launched. The Navy hoped that using a frisbee would keep a flare in the air for more time than the parachute design they were using. However, once the flare was attached to the frisbee, the extra weight caused the toy to flop back to the ground.

**VERDICT**
*Fact*

# PEOPLE LEARNED TO SURF BY RIDING DOLPHINS

## FACT OR FAKE?

Reports of the exciting activity 'surfing' began in the 1900s, and it soared in popularity in the 1960s. But its origins are much earlier. The roots of surfing can be traced to ancient Polynesia, in the Pacific Ocean where people surfed on wooden boards (not dolphins).

## TELL ME MORE

European explorers first described seeing Polynesian and Hawaiian people riding the waves in the early 18th century. However, as more people travelled to the islands, strict missionaries disapproved of the sport and stopped it. Boo!

### SURF DIARY

In 1778 Captain James Cook and his crew were the first Europeans to visit Hawaii and see people surfing. One of the crew's diaries reads:
*This man felt the most supreme pleasure, while he was driven on, so fast and so smoothly, by the sea.*

VERDICT
## Fake

Don't worry, I'll be gentle ...

# JUDO MEANS THE 'GENTLE WAY'

## FACT OR FAKE?

The martial art judo was formed as a self-defence system, but also a way of life. It includes physical, intellectual and moral aspects. *Ju* means 'gentle' and *do* means 'way or path'.

## TELL ME MORE

Judo was founded by Jigoro Kano in 1882, based on elements of Japanese jujitsu. Judo became popular and was incorporated into the Olympics in 1964. Judo is divided into three key moves: *nage waza* (throws), *katame waza* (controls) or *atami waza* (kicks). *Atami waza* are not allowed in competition.

VERDICT
Fact

91

# GLOSSARY

**advantage** – having a better chance than someone else

**agility** – being able to move easily and quickly

**catcher (baseball)** – the player positioned behind the batter, who catches the ball if the batter misses

**cavalry** – soldiers trained to fight and perform duties on horseback

**curling** – a game where players slide heavy stones along an ice sheet towards the end, marked as the 'house'

**debut** – a player's first appearance in a specific role

**decibel** – a unit used to measure sound

**decorum** – refined and appropriate behaviour

**deliberate** – to do something on purpose, not by accident

**disqualify** – to remove someone from a game or competition because they have broken a rule

**durable** – able to last and be used for a long time without becoming damaged

**eliminate** – remove from competition

**encase** – surround or cover in a tight coating

**FIFA** – Fédération Internationale de Football Association; the international governing body for football, based in Zurich, Switzerland

**FINA** – Fédération Internationale de Natation; the international governing body for swimming, water polo, diving, artistic swimming, open water swimming and high diving; based in Lausanne, Switzerland

**free kick (football)** – a kick awarded to a football team when the other team commits an offence; an indirect free kick must touch another player before a goal can be scored; a direct free kick can be used to score a goal straight away, with no other players involved

**gymnasium** – a room or building used for physical exercise

**inflammation** – a condition where part of the body becomes swollen, red, hot and/or sore as a result of damage or injury

**intestines** – a long tube through which food travels from the stomach and out of the body while it is being digested

**invasion** – when an army invades another country in an attempt to take over or occupy it

**lenient** – not too strict with rules; a lenient referee may let minor rule offences go without penalty to allow the game to flow

**mimic** – to copy or behave like something or someone else

**missionaries** – people who travel to spread religious thought and beliefs

**mosquito** – a long-legged fly that lays eggs in water; the female's blood-sucking bite can transfer harmful germs and disease

**NBA** – National Basketball Association, the professional basketball league in the USA

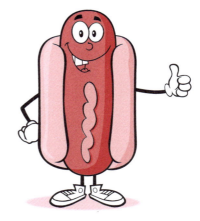

**Persians** – people who lived in or came from Persia, an ancient kingdom in south-western Asia, the central part of which was renamed Iran in 1935

**phenomenon** – something or someone that is remarkable or draws attention

**pitcher (baseball)** – the player who throws the ball to the batter

**polyester** – a type of plastic usually used to make fabric

**Polynesia** – a region in the central Pacific containing the islands of Hawaii, the Marquesas Islands, Samoa, the Cook Islands and French Polynesia

**retire** – to stop competing in sport competitions

# GLOSSARY (CONT)

**sabotage** – to deliberately damage something to help someone else

**set piece** – a planned and practised move or series of moves by a sports team

**shrapnel** – a piece of a bomb or other material thrown out by an explosion

**stamina** – to be able to keep going for a long time

**standardise** – to set out a standard measure or dimension for something that others must follow

**super-heavyweight** – a weight category in boxing above heavyweight; weight categories are used in boxing and other combat sports so that players fight other players of a similar weight to make sure the fight is fair

**sustainability** – acting in a way that avoids damaging or using up Earth's natural resources

**synchronise** – to time actions so that they happen at the same time

**tenacity** – to be determined

**timeout** – a brief break in play where the team and coaching staff can talk

**triathlon** – a race with three parts, usually swimming, running and cycling

**urn** – a pot or jar, usually used to store a dead person's ashes

**varsity** – the first team representing a school or college at a sport; junior varsity is the level below

**visible** – able to be seen

**vulcanisation** – a process that hardens rubber

# FURTHER INFORMATION

## BOOKS

**Sport (Go Quiz Yourself)**
by Annabel Savery, (Wayland 2020)

**Sports (Infomojis)**
by Jon Richards and Ed Simkins, (Wayland 2019)

**Incredible Sporting Champions (Brilliant Women)**
by Georgia Amson-Bradshaw, (Wayland 2019)

**Sport (Strange but True)**
by Nancy Dickmann, (Franklin Watts 2017)

**Women in Sport**
by Rachel Ignotofsky, (Wren & Rook 2018)

## WEBSITES

**https://olympics.com/en**
Learn all about the Olympics with latest news, history and
athlete statistics.

**http://news.bbc.co.uk/sport1/hi/academy/default.stm**
Find out the latest from your favourite sports and sports stars at
the Sport Academy page.

**www.rulesofsport.com**
Look up any sport on the Rules of Sport website to get a basic
introduction: the rules, equipment, objectives and scoring systems.

# INDEX

# Titles in the series

9781526318220

9781526318527

9781526318466

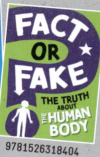

9781526318404

9781526318497

FACT OR FAKE — THE TRUTH ABOUT SCIENCE

9781526318442

FACT OR FAKE — THE TRUTH ABOUT SPACE

9781526318428

FACT OR FAKE — THE TRUTH ABOUT SPORTS

9781526318503

9781526318541

9781526318565